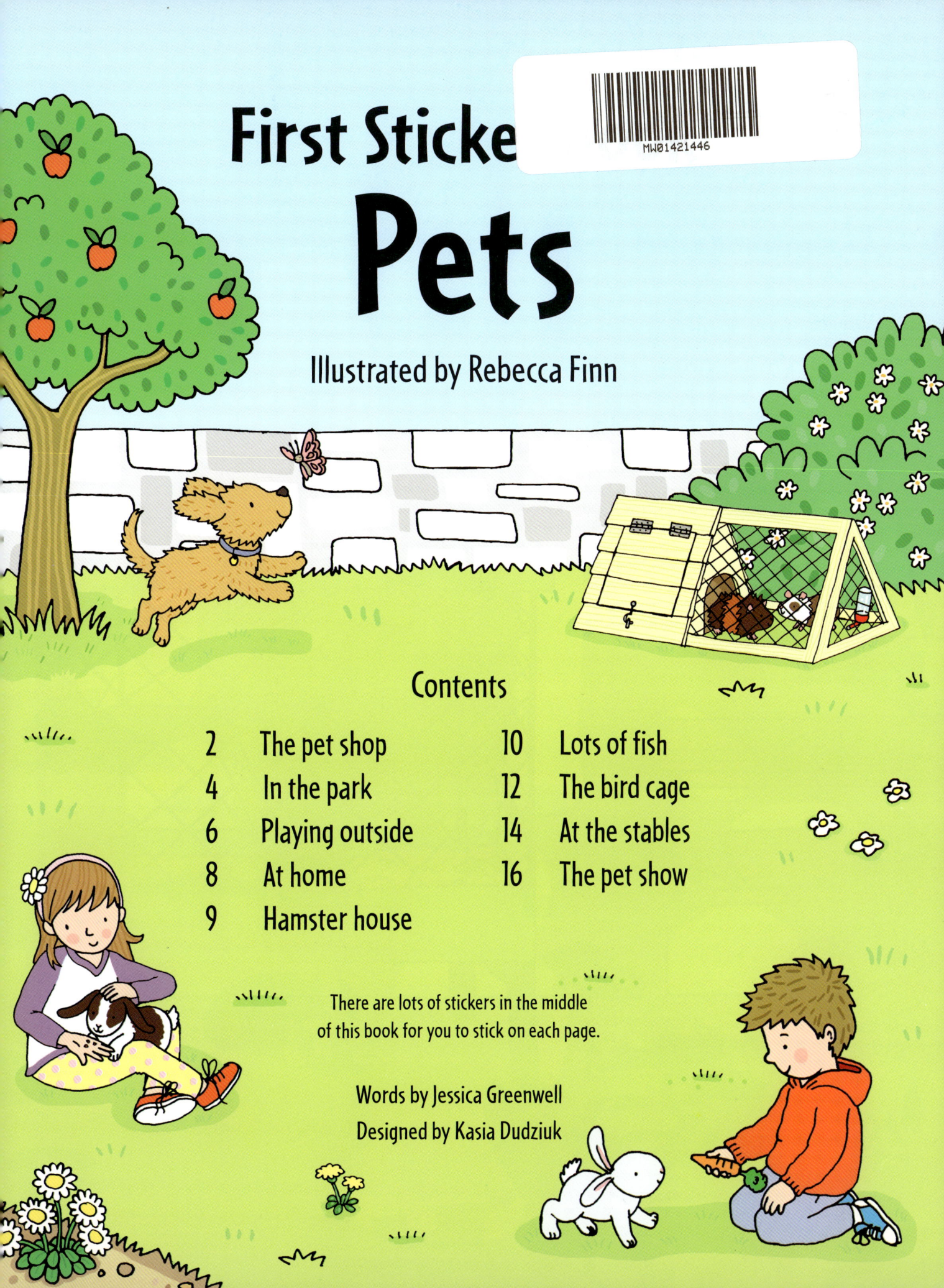

The pet shop

This pet shop sells all kinds of different animals. Can you put each one in the right place?

In the park

It's a sunny day in the park. Fill the picture with people walking their dogs.

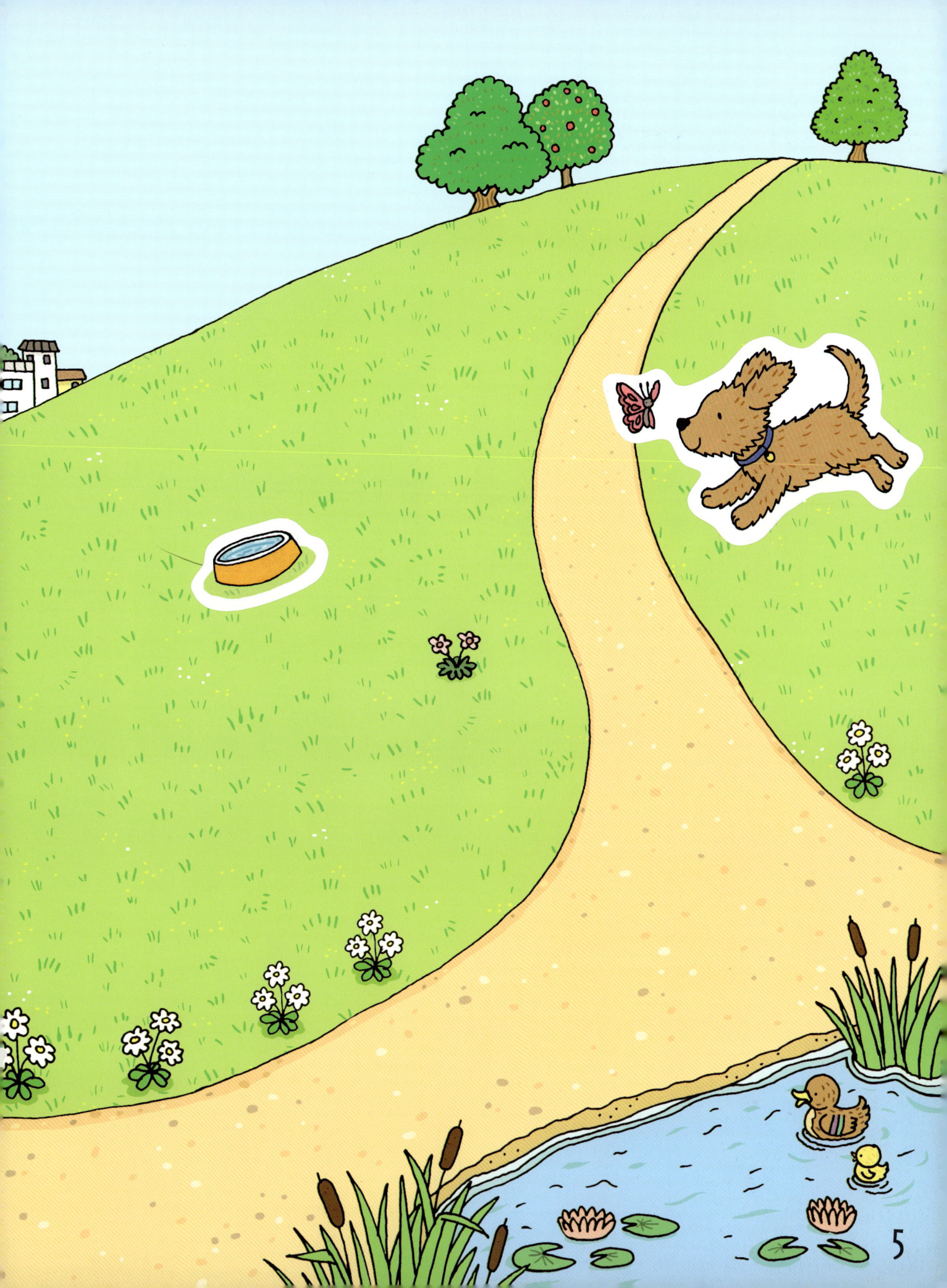

Playing outside

Pets love to be outside in the springtime. Put some hopping rabbits on the grass.

At home

Lots of pets live in this house. Find a place for some playful kittens and puppies.

The pet shop

Geckos

Mice   Tortoise

Chameleon

Tarantulas

Snake

Parrot

Chinchillas

In the park

Playing outside

At home

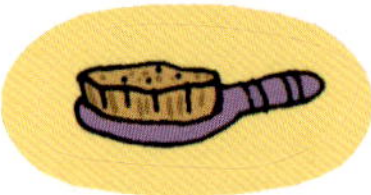

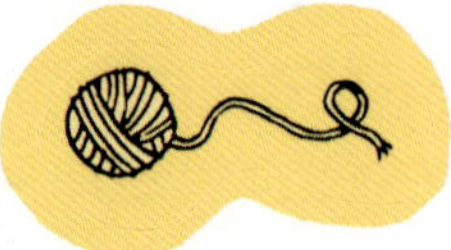

Hamster house

Lots of fish

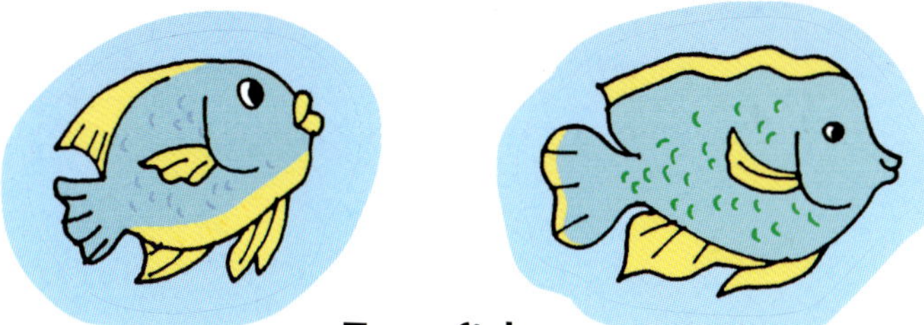

Angelfish

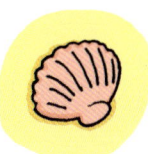

Tang fish

Butterfly fish

Clown fish

Sweetlips

Angelfish

Sea horses

Damselfish

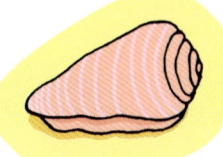

Longnose butterfly fish

Garibaldi fish

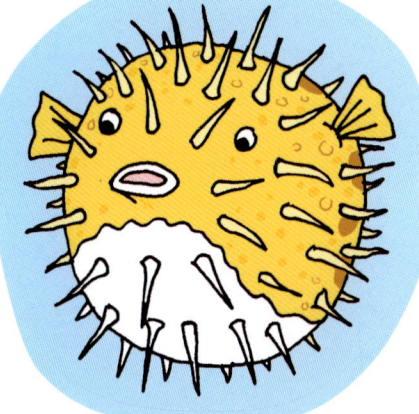
Puffer fish

The bird cage

At the stables

The pet show

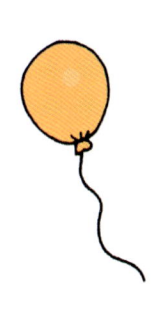

Hamster house

This is where hamsters eat, sleep and play.
Add some little hamsters to the picture.

Lots of fish

Fill this big tank with tropical fish.
Can you find a clown fish and a sea horse?

The bird cage

Lots of pretty birds live here. Where could you stick a bird looking in a mirror?

At the stables

Riders look after their ponies at the stables. Find a place for a boy grooming his pony.

The pet show

Lots of animals are winning prizes at this pet show. Put some prize-winning pets in the picture.